Published in 2013 by Helen Exley® Gifts in Great Britain.
Design, selection and arrangement © Helen Exley Creative Ltd 2013
This edition published 2014 for Index Books.

12 11 10 9 8 7 6 5 4 3 2 1

ISBN 978-1-84634-701-6

Helen Exley® Gifts,
16 Chalk Hill, Watford, Herts WD19 4BG, UK.
www.helenexley.com

Follow us on  and

Mothers&
Daughters

Illustrated by Juliette Clarke

A HELEN EXLEY GIFT BOOK

ABOUT THIS BOOK

Helen Exley, who created
Mothers & Daughters, lived thousands
of miles from her mother.
She phoned her every other day.
"I knew everything in her life,
and she was the same with me –
she even knew what
the weather was like here.
She meant the world to me.
That's why I love these quotes.
They say everything we'd all like to say
to someone who is so central,
so vital to our life."

CHAPTER 1

OUR
UNIQUE
BOND

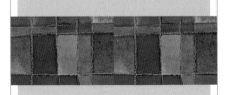

A daughter and
her mother…
are so entwined in heart
and mind that, gladly
or unwillingly, they share
each love, each joy,
each sorrow and each bitter
wrong lifelong.

PAM BROWN, B.1928

I T'S NOT FLESH
AND BLOOD,
BUT THE HEART
THAT MAKES US MOTHERS
AND DAUGHTERS.

AUTHOR UNKNOWN

...The daughter
never ever gives up
on the mother, just as the
mother never gives up
on the daughter.
There is a tie here so strong
that nothing can break it.
I called it "the
unbreakable bond".

RACHEL BILLINGTON, B.1942

We are all daughters of the present, with the potential to impact a new motherhood as well as a new womanhood. But… there always will be a unique tie between mother and daughter in our society.

PHYLLIS MAGRAB

M others of daughters
are daughters of mothers
and have remained so,
in circles joined to circles,
since time began.

SIGNE HAMMER

The relationship between a mother and her daughter is as varied, as mysterious, as constantly changing and interconnected as the patterns that touch, move away from, and touch again in a kaleidoscope.

LYN LIFSHIN

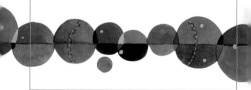

WHEN YOU ARE
A MOTHER, YOU ARE NEVER
REALLY ALONE IN YOUR
THOUGHTS. YOU ARE
CONNECTED TO YOUR
CHILD AND TO ALL THOSE
WHO TOUCH YOUR LIVES.

SOPHIA LOREN, B.1934

…two people
as deeply bound
to each other
as a mother and her
daughter are never
really separated,
even by death.

RITA RUDNER

Whether they realize it or not mothers and daughters are still entangled, even into age – and one's pain and joy lives in the other's heart.

PAM BROWN, B.1928

Mothers and
daughters are part
of each other's
consciousness,
in different degrees
and in a different

way, but still with
the mutual sense
of something
which has always
been there.

EDITH WHARTON

A mother
and her children have
a relationship different
to any other – whatever
loves, whatever hates,
lie between them,
they are bound together.

PAMELA DUGDALE

*L*ike it or not, we are bound
to one another. It is the lightest
of links — so light
that sometimes we seem
to forget it altogether.
But it is stronger than
life itself.

PAM BROWN, B.1928

...the relationship –
of Mother and Child
– remains incredible
and indestructible –
the strongest bond
upon this earth.

THEODOR REIK

CHAPTER 2

WHEN YOU WERE BORN...

...when they put
your first child into
your arms, perhaps you
will think of me – that it
was a high moment
in my life too when
for the first time I held
you, a little red bundle,
in my arms.

ROSE SCHLOSINGER
(1907-1943)

FROM THE INSTANT
I SAW HER... I LOVED HER
WITH AN INTENSITY THAT LIFE
HAD NOT PREPARED ME FOR.

SUSAN CHEEVER

*The times we spent together
took on a special intimacy,
a quality that I remember best
from the day I woke up and my
daughter was brought to me
in hospital. I won't top that
feeling in my lifetime.*

TAMMY GRIMES

SHE LOOKED UP AT ME.
THE CRYING STOPPED.
HER EYES MELTED
THROUGH ME, FORGING
A CONNECTION IN ME WITH
THEIR SOFT HEAT.

SHIRLEY MACLAINE, B.1934, FROM
"DANCE WHILE YOU CAN"

She was my firstborn.
No child was ever more
wanted, more adored.
I had a very special delight
in her, cuddly closeness
with her, and understanding
with her.

PATRICIA NEAL (1926-2010)

...my heart was all hers.
I was terrified, elated,
proud, and complete...
all at once... On that day...
we began our wonderful
duet, a blend of heart,
mind, and soul that
continues to this day.

NAOMI JUDD

*Y*our pain I could
not bear for you.
I could not remember
my pain for you.
Only the small life
in my arms — My girl,
my daughter — you.

BARBARA RENNIE

*S*pring, the birth
of nature; soft air filled
with the promise of
warmth, sun speckling
the ground and a
new young mother

*with her baby
daughter soothed and
asleep in her arms
under a tree. What
nicer piece of life?*

JANE-LOUISE MIDDLETON

CHAPTER 3

A DAUGHTER IS HER MOTHER

The most
sophisticated woman
has a streak
of her mother
running through her.

PAM BROWN, B.1928

...THE DAUGHTER
IS FOR
THE MOTHER
AT ONCE
HER DOUBLE
AND ANOTHER
PERSON.

SIMONE DE BEAUVOIR
(1908-1986), FROM
"THE SECOND SEX"

Just as you
inherit your mother's
brown eyes, you inherit
part of yourself.

ALICE WALKER, B.1944

As is the mother,

so is

her daughter.

EZEKIEL XVI: 44

*The woman who bore me
is no longer alive
but I seem to be her
daughter in increasingly
profound ways.*

JOHNETTA B. COLE

I am myself.
But I am of
your making.

PAM BROWN, B.1928

My love for her
and my hate for her are
so bafflingly intertwined
that I can hardly see her.
I never know who is who.
She is me and I am she
and we're all together.

ERICA JONG, B.1942

A daughter —
to her alarm —
is inclined to turn
into her mother,
however hard
she tries!

PAM BROWN, B.1928

I think a parent is always tougher on a child of the same sex – because they're us. Vanessa is exactly me: stubborn, independent-minded, emotional, quixotic, moody – and lacking in confidence.

JANE FONDA, B.1939

...you catch yourself in a gesture, a look, an expression that makes you think — "that's just like Ma". But it is also reassuring, for in the world of a million changes, it reaffirms the continuity of life, its eternal transmission and mystery.

MARY KENNY

*My daughters show
me myself. I am reflected
in their attitudes to others,
the way I relate to others
and especially in their
overall philosophy on life.
It's frightening and
flattering.*

MAUREEN MCGUIRE

Becoming my mother
is an odd process.
Sometimes I look in the
mirror, tracing the faint lines
that wind away from
the corners of my eyes,
like tributary rivers on a map.
I am, I realize, the best
memento I have of her.

ZOE HELLER, B.1965

CHAPTER 4

A LIFE
TO SHARE

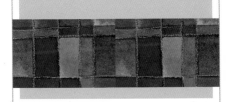

Mother darling,
It is wonderful to meet
and talk over everything
and share and laugh
and understand each
other's situations as
no one else can.

ANNE MORROW LINDBERGH
(1906-2001)

Mothers and daughters delight in each other's adventures.

PAMELA DUGDALE

Sales are largely
supported by mothers
and daughters looking
for surprises for
each other.

PAM BROWN, B.1928

*W*ithin minutes,
we're peddling away, the two
of us, a genetic sewing machine
that runs on limitless love.
It's my belief that between
mothers and daughters there is
a kind of blood-hyphen that is,
finally, indissoluble.

CAROL SHIELDS

We ring each other to say, "Goodnight, God bless," and, "Good morning". If she rings me first, I know it's to see if I'm still alive. We never stop laughing and we never stop crying when we are together.

THORA HIRD

Every now and again
one needs a day out
with Mum. Cream cakes,
small, silly extravagances.
Shoes off in the train.

PAM BROWN, B.1928

...TALKING
IS WHAT MOTHERS
LOVE TO DO
WITH THEIR
DAUGHTERS.

ANN F. CARON

It is a bonus to living
if a mother and daughter
know each other's size
and exactly what suits
the other.

PAM BROWN, B.1928

I wonder if you remember
how we loved long days in the
country? ...How we all put
on our bright gloves and went
crunching into the snow?
...Your tiny boots?
I remember. I always will.

HELEN THOMSON, B.1943

The trouble with mothers
is that however
well groomed and
sophisticated you appear
to strangers, *they* know
your knickers are probably
held up with a safety pin.

SAMANTHA ARMSTRONG

CHAPTER 5

HOLDING EACH OTHER UP

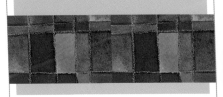

However hard life is for a mother she must show her children a steady and unchanging love — for this is the root of all the happiness they'll ever know.

PAM BROWN, B.1928

*W*hen I'm not tranquil,
she will try to steady me.
In my periods of loneliness,
she reassures me. What a
marvellous daughter she is!
Such humanity.

ROMILDA VILLANI, FROM
"SOPHIA: LIVING AND LOVING"

A baby girl sees her mother as wrap-around love. The first reproach astounds her but she learns... that love is constant whatever else changes.

PAM BROWN, B.1928

Thank you for giving
me the things I needed
to be a strong mother
– your love and support.
I love you, Boog!

LARAMIE,
TO HER DAUGHTER RACHELLE

I HAVE LEARNED TO
REALLY HEAR THE MESSAGE
MY MOTHER HAS GIVEN ME ALL
MY LIFE: "I WILL BE WITH YOU
ALWAYS." AS IN FOREVER,
INTO THE ETERNAL HEREAFTER,
NO MATTER WHAT.

REBECCA WALKER,
DAUGHTER OF ALICE WALKER

...whenever I have been upset... Leslie's the one I have unloaded on... An awful burden to have placed on her. I apologize to you publicly, my darling daughter.

LAUREN BACALL, B.1924

Her open mouth
groping on my cheek…
what pleasure, it is
almost a pain of happiness
to feel her oneness

with me, her absolute
dependence on me,
and her knowledge
that it is well for her
that she has me.

HELEN THOMAS

...your relationship with
your daughters is one you
can rely on, there for life,
an ongoing, developing
relationship. And it feels good
to know your children
know they can rely on you.

ENID JOHNS

I<small>T IS SUCH A PRIVILEGE</small>
<small>TO GROW WITH YOU,</small> J<small>ODIE.</small>
I <small>WILL TRY TO ENCOURAGE YOU</small>
<small>TO FACE UP TO HARD THINGS,</small>
<small>AND PLEASE WILL YOU ENCOURAGE</small>
<small>ME TO DO THE SAME?</small>

<small>SUSAN, TO HER DAUGHTER JODIE</small>

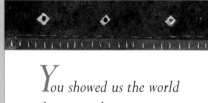

You showed us the world
and now we share your joy...
*You can never be lonely
— for our love is always
with you. Reach out to us
and we are there. As you have
always been for us.*

PAM BROWN, B.1928

As we move off into
the future, two separate women
each struggling to complete
herself, I know that we will
reach out to each other.
In my strength I can be a tree
for you to lean against.

RITA FREEMAN

CHAPTER 6

DAUGHTERS!

My daughter and I have
fiery red spats of argument;
intense crimson anger,
over and done with in minutes.
My husband, her father,
is open-mouthed at the love
after the storm.

EVIE BARBARELLI

One is never dull
with daughters...
Sometimes a little
dull seems totally
desirable.

PAM BROWN, B.1928

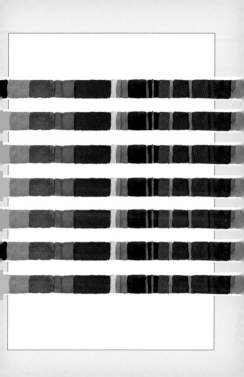

Rather suspiciously the words "I didn't..." were often uttered before the question was ever asked.

GIOVANNI ANDRETTI

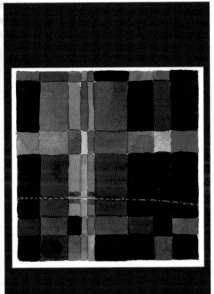

MOTHERS SPEND A LOT
OF TIME COMPARING NOTES
WITH OTHER MOTHERS
— ABOUT THE SUCCESSES
AND LUNATIC DECISIONS
OF THEIR DAUGHTERS.

PAM BROWN, B.1928

She is inventive,
original and takes what
she wants from life
– including many of her
mother's clothes.

RACHEL BILLINGTON, B.1942

Traditionally small boys bring
gifts of snails, dead sparrows,
stones and abandoned cogwheels
to their mothers. Small girls
bring wild flowers...
That is delusion! It is far more
likely to be a frog...
Or iridescent beetle.

PAMELA DUGDALE

*D*aughters are
a delight.
Some of the time.
Most of the time.
When, that is,
they are not

*putting their
white ballet tights
into the wash
inside black jeans.*

PAM BROWN, B.1928

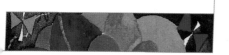

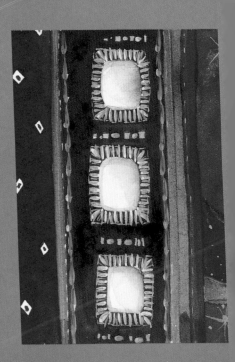

Telephones were invented 'specially for daughters.

LINDA MACFARLANE, B.1953

One must cling
to the back of the belief
that The Teens Will Pass.

PAM BROWN, B.1928

There's nothing
wrong with teenagers
that reasoning
with them won't
aggravate.

AUTHOR UNKNOWN

THERE IS NOTHING
THAT SO PIQUES
A DAUGHTER
AS A MOTHER'S
WARNING TURNING
OUT TO BE JUSTIFIED.

PAM BROWN, B.1928

CHAPTER 7

IN TIMES OF TROUBLE

A mother's best reward
is if her daughter turns to
her in times of trouble
— and shares with her
discoveries and dreams.

PAM BROWN, B.1928

Mothers learn
very early that daughters
will do as daughters do
– and all a mother
can do is stand by to
pick up the pieces.

PAMELA DUGDALE

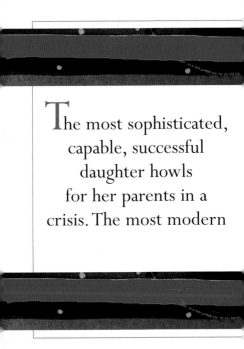

The most sophisticated,
capable, successful
daughter howls
for her parents in a
crisis. The most modern

and socially involved
mother or father
will drop everything
to rush to a daughter
in trouble.

JANET M. BRIDGES

DAUGHTER TO
MOTHER:
MOTHER, I HAVE
WORN YOUR NAME
LIKE A SHIELD.
IT HAS TORN BUT
PROTECTED ME
ALL THESE YEARS...

LUCILLE CLIFTON

When in doubt,
when in trouble,
a daughter swears
she will not run
for home.
But usually does
in the end.

PAM BROWN, B.1928

I wrapped you
in protection,
yet each time telling myself,
"Teach her to clad herself
in armor and be brave.
I must remember
to love her enough
to let her fall."

DONNA GREEN

Anything that happens, you can confide in Mama. Mama loves each child the way God loves His children. Nothing's

too bad to tell Mama.
Don't ever tell
me a lie. It's not
necessary, because
Mama will understand.

NANNY JAMES LOGAN DELANY

Sometimes the greatest comfort is to return to the nest and be a little child again. Hot-water bottles, tea and sympathy.

PAMELA DUGDALE

Parents, however old
they and we may grow to be,
serve among other things to
shield us from a sense of our
doom. As long as they are
around, we can avoid the fact
of our own mortality; we can
still be innocent children.

JANE HOWARD,
FROM "A DIFFERENT WOMAN"

I never cease to be
astonished that you survive
my moods, my stupidities,
my incredible mistakes
— that you accept my foibles.
Sometimes I think
"If I were you, I'd run a mile
from me" — but you never do.

PAM BROWN, B.1928

WHAT DO GIRLS
DO WHO HAVEN'T
ANY MOTHERS TO
HELP THEM THROUGH
THEIR TROUBLES?

LOUISA MAY ALCOTT
(1832-1888)

If there is anything
in my life that can be
of value to you,
I want you to have it;
if I can save you
a stumble or
a single false step,
I want to do it.

FLORENCE
WENDEROTH SAUNDERS

What would be given
to you if I had the power?
Cash to tide you over
the bad times? Valuable
introductions? Sound advice?
Maybe, though, what I have
is best – love and the promise
that I'm always here.

PAM BROWN, B.1928

To a child
a mother must
be a sure and
certain refuge —
all through
her life.

CHARLOTTE GRAY

CHAPTER 8

LETTING HER FLY FREE

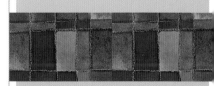

Life... would give
her everything of
consequence,
life would shape her,
not we. All we were
good for was to
make the
introductions.

HELEN HAYES (1900-1993)

*Mothers start our lives.
They cast on our existence...
They give us the basic patterns.
But the good ones... hand over
the needles after a while,
and say: "There's the world,
Love. Choose yourself some new
shades, some new patterns.
Make yourself a life."*

PAM BROWN, B.1928

What I wanted most
for my daughter was
that she be able to soar
confidently in her
own sky, wherever
that might be…

HELEN CLAES

The very essence
of motherly love
is to care for the
child's growth,
and that means
to want the child's
separation from
herself.

ERICH FROMM (1900-1980)

My mother wanted
me to be her wings,
to fly as she never quite
had the courage to do.
I love her for that. I love
the fact that she wanted
to give birth to her
own wings.

ERICA JONG, B.1942

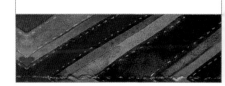

*You are free at last
— not held by obligation.
Only by love. Move out
into the wider world.
Treasure all that life
offers you in splendid
pleasures and in rich
experience.*

PAM BROWN, B.1928

We have to let go their hands. But the joys we knew before, remembered or lost, are part of us all forever.

PAMELA DUGDALE

CHAPTER 9

TIME APART

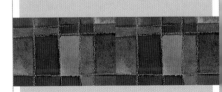

When a mother
and daughter have
plenty to share,
they can be many
miles apart and yet
be close.

SHEILA KITZINGER, B.1929,
FROM
"BECOMING A GRANDMOTHER"

Having been fashioned
from me, all you do
— despite your freedom
— must affect me too.

And so when we're apart,
I will always long for news
from you.

MAYA V. PATEL, B.1943

*I*n the dark hours before
dawn, I read your
last letter, full of plans
and adventures. And the past
falls into perspective.

PAM BROWN, B.1928

Love me always
and forever, my existence
depends on it...
you are all my joy
and all my sorrow.
What remains of my life

is overshadowed
by grief when
I consider how much
of it will be spent far
from you.

MADAME MARIE DE SÉVIGNÉ
(1626-1696)

A mother learns to take
postcards with equanimity.
"Bangkok. Been in local
hospital but OK now.
May go North at the end
of the week. Not sure where
to, but will let you know
if and when I find a P.O. Love
to all. Especially the cat."

PAM BROWN, B.1928

MOTHER'S VOICE
CLINGS TO MY HEART
LIKE TRAILS
OF BEDSTRAW
THAT CATCH YOU
IN THE LANES.

MARY WEBB

MOTHERS AND DAUGHTERS ENCHANT EACH OTHER,

WITH A HUNDRED MILES BETWEEN THEM.

PAM BROWN, B.1928

CHAPTER 10

MOTHERS!

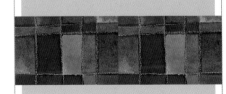

A daughter lives
in constant fear that
her mother will get out
the photograph album
and tell her all about
that Channel crossing
in graphic detail.

PAM BROWN, B.1928

If an experience in childhood still brings an agony of embarrassment – one's mother is guaranteed to relate it at a dinner for the in-laws!

PAMELA DUGDALE

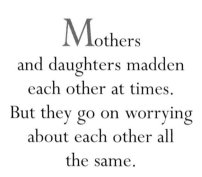

Mothers
and daughters madden
each other at times.
But they go on worrying
about each other all
the same.

PAM BROWN, B.1928

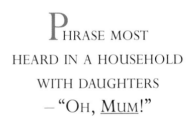

PHRASE MOST
HEARD IN A HOUSEHOLD
WITH DAUGHTERS
– "OH, MUM!"

CHARLOTTE GRAY

Mothers mean not to — but they can't help slipping in a word of advice.

MARION C. GARRETTY
(1917-2005)

Grandmas can make funnier faces and more awful noises than mothers. Mothers say it's because they've lost their inhibitions. And sometimes they just say "Mum!"

PAM BROWN, B.1928

CHAPTER 11

THAT GREAT LOVE

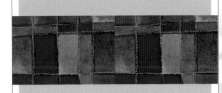

From the moment
I saw you I knew that
we were meant to do great
things in life, together.
I love you as much as
any mother could love
her child.

JENNIFER,
TO HER DAUGHTER KALLYSTA

You pause,
just ready to grow up.
Your smile says — I will
be a woman like you,
my smile says,

you are pure delight.
In that flash
of love and homage
we know it is sweet to
be female.

CHRISTINE CRAIG,
FROM "ISLAND"

Mothers give their
love and care and never
ask for repayment.
But rejoice if that love
is returned.

PAM BROWN, B.1928

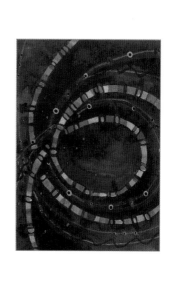

A mother
and daughter may stop
talking to each other
but they can never stop
loving each other.

LINDA MACFARLANE,
B.1953

My first thought
of you is of overwhelming,
overflowing love.
An unconditional love,
born out of your being
my firstborn, my vulnerable,
disabled daughter.

WENDY, TO HER DAUGHTER JAIME,
WHO HAS A RARE GENETIC DISEASE

Wherever you are
– in city street or in the
hush and glimmer of
a summer wood – our love
is with you. It shines
in the quiet pool. It wheels
above you in the flight
of swallows.

CHARLOTTE GRAY

A mother may sigh
to see her baby grow into
a schoolchild, a schoolchild
into an undergraduate,
an undergraduate into a
professional – with a life
and loves all her own.
But she loves her exactly
the same.

PAM BROWN, B.1928

Even when you did
something terribly
naughty like pull
the cat's tail
— just saying your name
caused me to smile
and made it impossible
to be cross.

LINDA MACFARLANE, B.1953

I suspect I have been a disappointment in a lot of ways… Scarcely the dream you dreamed when I was very small. And yet, you couldn't have loved me more. Or I you.

PAMELA DUGDALE

A mother loves her
children as they are now –
the sum of all the ages she
has known and loved.
She's saved the shadows
of those days – the

drawings, the gifts,
the letters – and treasures
them. But she loves best
what is here and now
– and awaits the future
with a happy heart.

PAM BROWN, B.1928

CHAPTER 12

OUR
MEMORIES...

I've got a beautiful wooden box for my necklaces and rings, but my real treasures are inside an old baby milk tin. There you'll find your hospital baby bracelet, your first shoe, a lock of hair… your first drawing, your first story…

LINDA MACFARLANE,
B.1953

I keep an album
of photographs of you
– as if I could hold on
to all the different yous
– the baby, the toddler,
the schoolgirl,
the teenager…
you are all of them –
and every time
I see you I think,
"This is the best time."

PAM BROWN, B.1928

Your first swan.
Your first day by the sea.
In sharing your childhood
discoveries,
I have relived my own.

MARION C. GARRETTY
(1917-2005)

I will always
hold the memories
of your childhood
– but will not
regret their

passing – for every
day you bring
me new
astonishments.

PAM BROWN, B.1928

It's good when a mother
and her daughter...
store things in their
minds to tell each other.
People they've met,
things they've done,

delights…
Small threads that
bind them together
in love and
understanding.

CHARLOTTE GRAY

CHAPTER 13

ALL MY MOTHER GAVE ME

MY MOTHER
TAUGHT ME TO
WALK PROUD AND TALL
"AS IF THE WORLD
WAS MINE".

SOPHIA LOREN, B.1934

*...the walks and talks
we have with our
two-year-olds in red boots
have a great deal to do
with the values they will
cherish as adults.*

EDITH F. HUNTER
(1919-2012)

I had very strong women role models in my mother, my grandmother, and my aunt. They used to say, "When you fall down again, get up. And don't be ashamed of falling down."

CARRIE SAXON PERRY

A loving and careful mother both recognizes and even protects her daughter's autonomy and also helps her dance out confidently on to a wider stage.

RACHEL BILLINGTON, B.1942,
FROM "THE GREAT UMBILICAL"

A woman learns
at her mother's knee
to love and trust,
to rejoice in life
and to go forward
with confidence
and hope.

PAM BROWN, B.1928

I miss her all the time.
Her voice, her smile,
her love, her wisdom.
But I feel a part of her
has merged with me. I know
what she'd think: "Go for it..."
And she's given me the
freedom to do just that.

CAROLE STONE, FROM
"THE DAILY TELEGRAPH",
MARCH 3, 1995

And as I grew
she shared good
times with me.
She taught me
to be realistic
and understanding,

she taught me how
a mother should be,
but most importantly,
she taught me how
to be a woman.

DEBRA DUEL, AGE 15

Chapter 14

A Daughter's Gift

Daughters

were to give

mothers

A sense of

themselves.

SINDAMANI BRIDGLAL,
FROM "SHE LIVES BETWEEN
BACK HOME AND HOME"

...it was my daughter
who often seemed most
meaningful in my struggle
for my lost Self.
She was my little Echo,
my "mirror," the answer
to a mother's dreams.

COLETTE DOWLING,
FROM "PERFECT WOMEN"

E VERY MOTHER...
HAS A DRAWER FULL OF
EXTRAORDINARY GIFTS
DONATED BY HER
DAUGHTERS OVER A
LIFETIME. ALL PRISTINE.
ALL TREASURED.

PAM BROWN, B.1928

*E*very ounce of love
a mother gives to
her child nourishes,
reinforces, encourages,
and teaches not only
her child but herself.

ALEXANDRA STODDARD

You have such an effect
on my emotions, giving me
a new range of them. I never
thought I could love so much
or hurt so badly for another
person. It's impossible to
tell you just how much you
mean to me.

JENNIFER, TO HER DAUGHTER KALLYSTA

Because of you,
I see every day
with a clearer eye
— as if for the
very first time.

PAM BROWN, B.1928

CHAPTER 15

SO PROUD, SO PROUD

My proudest pleasure
is when my beautiful
little three-year-old girl
puts her arms around
my neck, she squeezes me
tight and says, "I love you
Mummy, I really do."

A. COOPER

It does not matter
what my ending is – for
I have given the world my
daughters, and they are a
treasure beyond all price.

PAM BROWN, B.1928

*M*others who admire
their daughters are
the luckiest women in
the world. Thank you
for making me the luckiest
of the lucky.

LINDA MACFARLANE

*O*ne thing remember,
my girls… both of us trust
and hope that our daughters,
whether married or single,
will be the pride and
comfort of our lives.

LOUISA MAY ALCOTT
(1832-1888)

CHAPTER 16

THANK YOU TO A MOST SPECIAL MOTHER

Let me thank you
for all the times that
I forgot to thank you –
taking your love,
your patience and
forgiveness for granted.

PAM BROWN, B.1928

Whenever I had a broken heart, you healed that with kindness… Whenever my dreams didn't come true, you replaced the void with kindness. Thank goodness, your kindness never seems to run out.

SIÂN E. MORGAN, B.1973

*S*ure I love the dear silver
that shines in your hair.
And the brow that's all
furrowed, and wrinkled
with care. I kiss the dear
fingers, so toilworn for me.

RIDA JOHNSON YOUNG
FROM THE SONG
"MOTHER MACHREE"

The best thing about getting old, Mum says, is that your children have forgiven you. Forgive me, too, Mum. Age teaches us that we are simply human.

PAM BROWN, B.1928

The little things that I never really noticed all come back now as I have my own daughter. Thanks, Mom, for being such a strong model for me. You made it seem easy.

MEREDITH RALSTON

CHAPTER 17

DEVOTED TO MY LOVELY GIRL

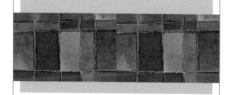

Having
a daughter
I like is the best
thing
that's happened
to me.

AUTHOR UNKNOWN,
FROM "GOOD HOUSEKEEPING"

You came third
in the one hundred
metres, second in the
long jump, but always
first in my heart.

LINDA MACFARLANE, B.1953

I would tear down a star
and put it into a smart jewelry
box if I could.
I would seal up love
in a long thin bottle so that
you could sip it whenever
it was needed if I could.

ANNE SEXTON

I already begin to be devoured
with expectation. I hope for
no consolation but from your
letters and yet I know they will
only make me sigh still more deeply.
In short, my dear child,
I live but for you.

MADAME MARIE DE SÉVIGNÉ
(1626-1696)

How can one say
no to a child?
How can one be
anything but a slave
to one's own flesh
and blood?

HENRY MILLER
(1891-1980)

In the lottery
of my life,
my daughter
is the six numbers
— and the bonus.

AUTHOR UNKNOWN

*S*he laughs when I laugh,
she cries when I cry,
she lives when I live.
I can't say more about
her except that she lives
for me and I live for her.

JOSEPHIDES PANAYIOTA,
AGE 16

Dearest daughter.
One tiny tug will have me
dropping any masterpiece
on which I am engaged
– you are, above everything,
the heartbeat of my life.

PAM BROWN, B.1928

CHAPTER 18

FRIENDS FOR LIFE

I loved my baby,
I loved my budding
ballet dancer, I loved
my argumentative
adolescent. But most of all
I love the friend that my
daughter has become.

LINDA MACFARLANE,
B.1953

THERE COMES
A TIME WHEN
A MOTHER
AND DAUGHTER
ARE TWO
WOMEN TOGETHER.

PAM BROWN, B.1928

*T*here is a point
where you aren't
as much mom and
daughter as you are
adults and friends.

JAMIE LEE CURTIS,
B.1959

We live separate
lives now – but sometimes
we need each other as we did
when you were small
and we reach out…
and each is young again.

PAM BROWN, B.1928

We are friends.
We have loads
of fun together,
and our grooves continue
to sew the years into
a beautiful tapestry.

ALEXANDRA STODDARD

…she is a wise, giving, deeply loving daughter and friend. The chasm that existed between us is now, thankfully, a meadowland of conversation and love.

DEBBIE REYNOLDS

WHEN MOTHERS AND DAUGHTERS ARE FRIENDS, THE WORLD IS A BETTER PLACE.

LINDA MACFARLANE, B.1953

If you had never been born
this planet would be a little
colder, a little more drab
and dull… you have brought
laughter to our lives,
and kindliness and caring.
Through your eyes we've
discovered wonders from your
hands, the gift of friendship.

PAM BROWN, B.1928

I EVEN LOVE
HER BONES.
WE ARE SO CLOSE.
SHE IS MY
VERY BEST FRIEND.

FAITH BROWN

WHAT IS A
HELEN EXLEY® GIFT BOOK?

Helen Exley has been creating gift books
for more than twenty-seven years, and her
readers have bought more than 90 million
copies of her work in thirty-seven languages.

Because her books are bought as gifts,
she spares no expense in making sure that
each book is as thoughtful and meaningful
a gift as it is possible to create:
good to give, good to receive.

Team members help to find thoughtful
quotations from literally hundreds of sources,
and then the books are personally created.
With infinite care, Helen ensures that each
spread is individually designed to enhance
the feeling of the words and that the whole
book has real depth and meaning.

ACKNOWLEDGEMENTS:

The publishers are grateful for permission to reproduce
copyright material. Whilst every reasonable effort
has been made to trace copyright holders,
the publishers would be pleased to hear from any not
here acknowledged.

IMPORTANT COPYRIGHT NOTICE:

Text: Giovanni Andretti, Samantha Armstrong,
Pam Brown, Pamela Dugdale, Helen Exley,
Marion C. Garretty,
Charlotte Gray, Peter Gray, Linda Macfarlane,
Siân E. Morgan,
Maya V. Patel and
Helen Thomson are all
© Helen Exley Creative Ltd 2013.

Illustrations by Juliette Clarke:
© Helen Exley Creative Ltd 2013.

Helen Exley® Gifts
16 Chalk Hill,
Watford, Herts
WD19 4BG, UK

www.helenexley.com

Follow us on and